Picture and Figure Series

Book Cover by: Carol Hampshire
Illustrations by: Kenneth Sommer
Written and published by: Bright Kids NYC

Copyright © 2011 by Bright Kids NYC Inc. All of the questions in this book have been created by the staff and consultants of Bright Kids NYC Inc.

Bright Kids NYC Inc.
225 Broadway, Suite 3104
New York, NY 10007
www.brightkidsnyc.com
twitter.com/brightkidsnyc
info@brightkidsnyc.com
917-539-4575

About Bright Kids NYC

Bright Kids NYC was founded in New York City to provide language arts and math enrichment for young children and to educate parents about standardized tests through workshops and consultations, as well as to prepare young children for such tests through assessments, tutoring, and publications. Our philosophy is that, regardless of age, test-taking is a skill that can be acquired and mastered through practice.

At Bright Kids NYC, we strive to provide the best learning materials. Our publications are truly unique. First, our books have been written by qualified psychologists, learning specialists, and teachers. Second, our books have been tested by hundreds of children in our tutoring practice. Since children can make associations that many adults cannot, testing of materials by children is critical to creating successful publications. Finally, our learning specialists and teaching staff have provided practical strategies and tips so parents can best help their child prepare to compete successfully on standardized tests.

Feel free to contact us should you have any questions.

Bright Kids NYC Inc.
225 Broadway, Suite 3104
New York, New York 10007

Phone: 917-539-4575

Email: info@brightkidsnyc.com
www.brightkidsnyc.com
twitter.com/brightkidsnyc

Picture and Figure Series

Introduction

Picture and figure series questions involve determining the underlying rule of a series, and then applying the same rule to predict what will come next in the series. Many children confuse patterns with picture and figure series questions. The biggest difference between patterns and series is that while patterns always repeat themselves, questions involving picture and figure series always progress over time without repeating the actual picture or the figure itself.

There are several types of picture series questions:

1. Change in visual images over the progression of time, such as a decreasing amount of water in a glass, or progression of what a fruit might look like while it is being eaten.

2. Life cycle of various events such as trees losing leaves or snowmen melting over time.

3. Increase or decrease in size in one or more pictured objects.

4. Increase or decrease in quantity of one or more pictured objects.

Depicted below is a typical example of a pictures series question:

There are several types of figure series questions:

1. Increase or decrease in size of one or more figures.

2. Increase or decrease in quantity of one or more figures.

3. Movement or rotation of one or more figures.

4. Change in shade/color of one or more figures.

5. Addition or removal of one or more figures.

Figure series questions become more complex when there is more than one variable that changes, such as when one or more figures change in shade at the same time one or more figures increase in quantity. Children typically struggle with more figure series questions than picture series questions, thus we have included more figure series questions in this book.

Depicted below is a typical example of a figure series questions:

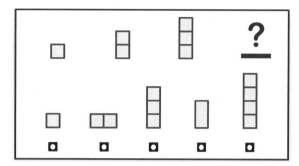

Picture and figure series questions improve children's problem solving skills and thus improve a child's critical thinking skills. Picture and figure series questions are also on many tests such as the Stanford-Binet, ERB/WISC-IV, and the OLSAT®.

How to Use this Book

This book is a practice guide for figure and picture series questions and it is divided into two sections. There are a total of 90 picture and figure series questions.

The first part of the book has picture series questions. There are 40 questions in this section. The second part of the book has figure series questions. There are 50 questions in this section. The final part of the book includes answer keys for picture and figure series questions.

Please be aware that figural series are particularly difficult for most children and this book should be paced based on the child's ability. Thus, it is important to work through problems slowly, and to provide positive reinforcement along the way. It is also important for children to verbalize the series, prior to picking an answer. By verbalizing the series, they understand the underlying rule for the series. Finally, simply being familiar with the format and rationale of series questions can help a child eliminate incorrect answers quickly.

Picture and Figure Series

Section One

Picture Series

Picture and Figure Series

1

2

3

4

Picture and Figure Series

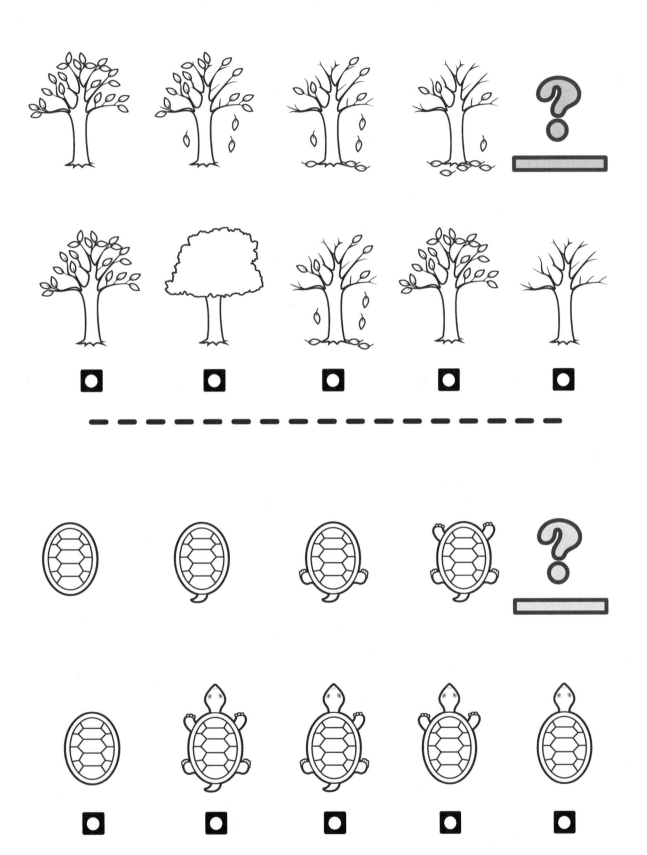

7

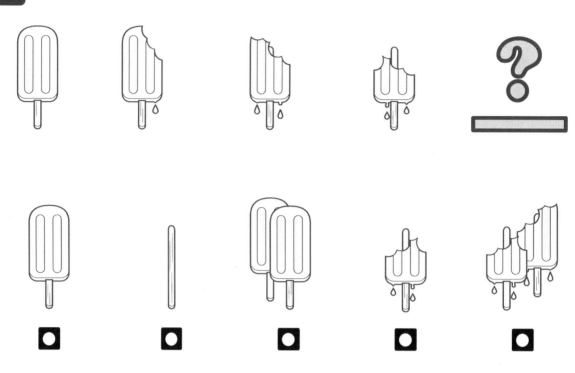

8

Picture and Figure Series

9

10

 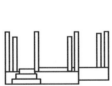 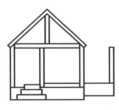 

 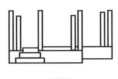   

11

    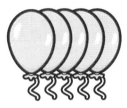

12

Picture and Figure Series

13

14

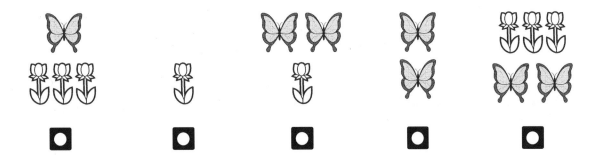

- - - - - - - - - - - - - - - - - - - -

Picture and Figure Series

17

18

19

20

Picture and Figure Series

21

 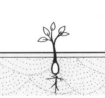  

22

23

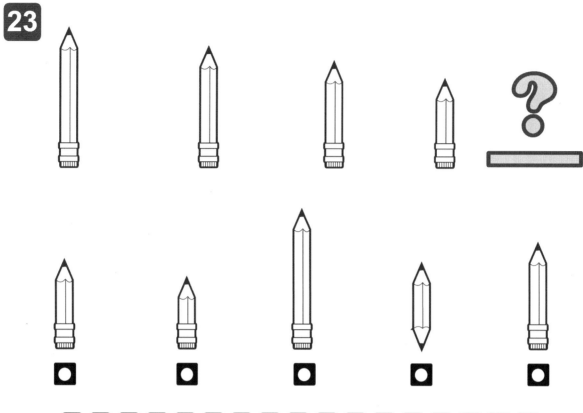

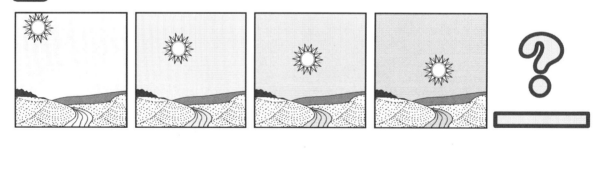

24

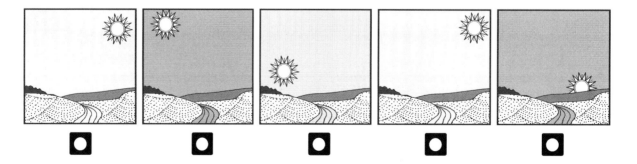

Picture and Figure Series

25

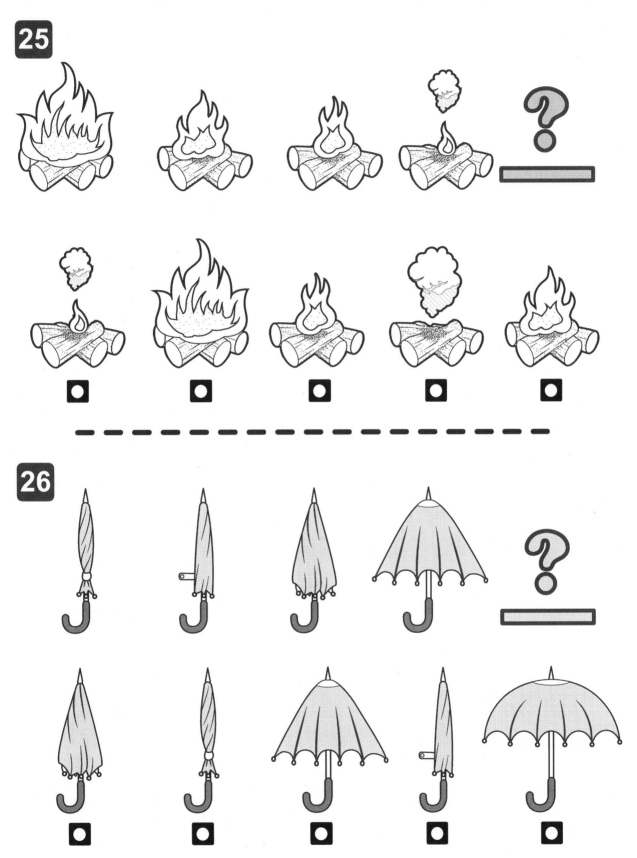

27

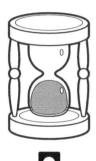    

28

    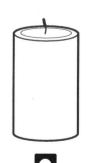

　Picture and Figure Series

29

30

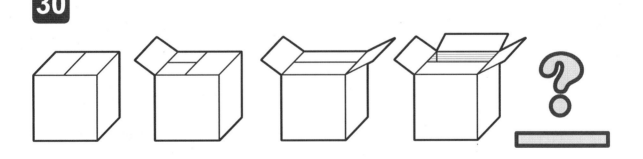

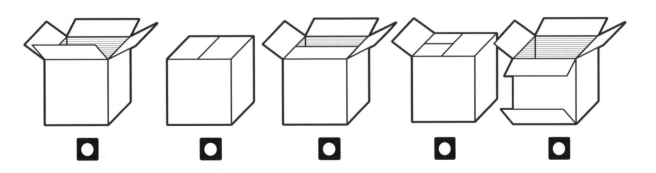

Section Two

Figure Series

Picture and Figure Series

1

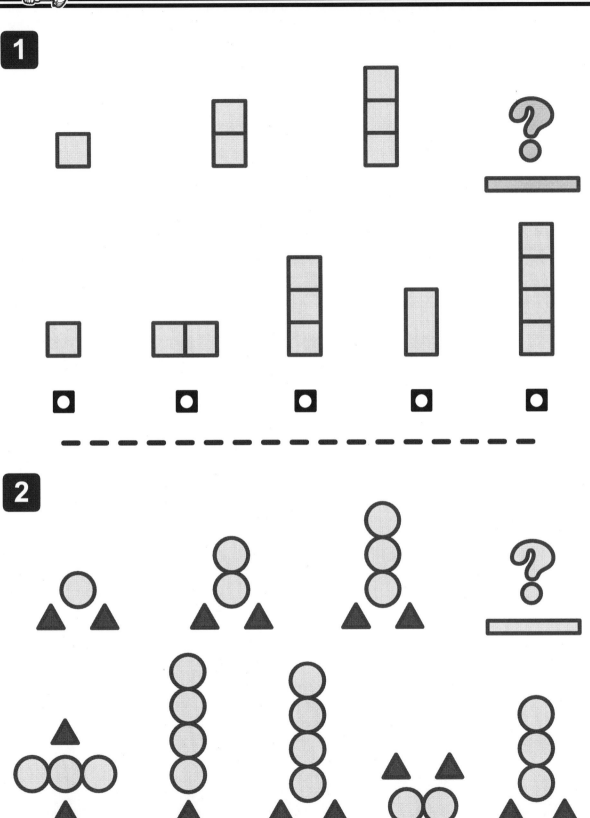

2

3

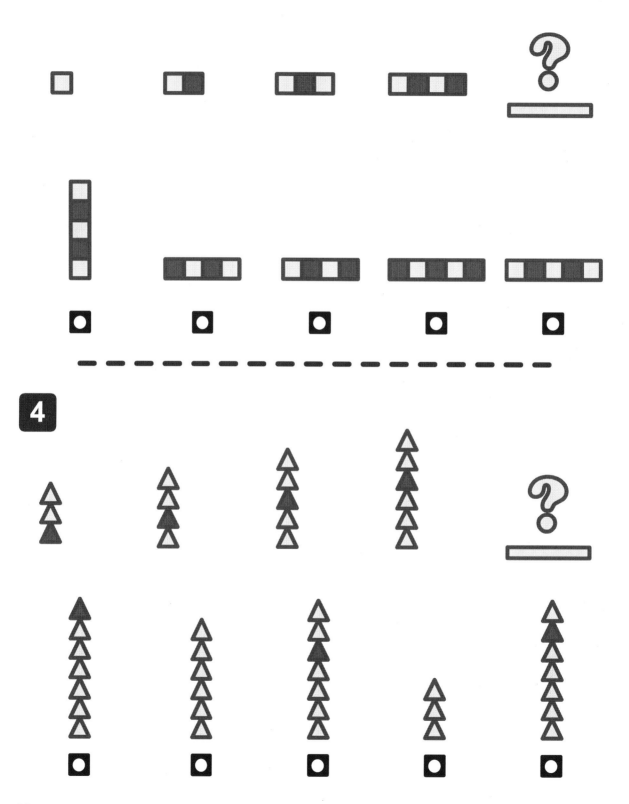

4

Picture and Figure Series

5

- -

6

7

1A   2B   3C   4D   5E
‗‗‗‗‗‗‗‗‗

5F   7F   6E   6F   7E
▫   ▫   ▫   ▫   ▫

- -

8

‗‗‗‗‗‗‗‗‗

9

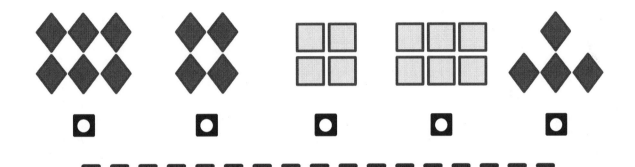

10

11

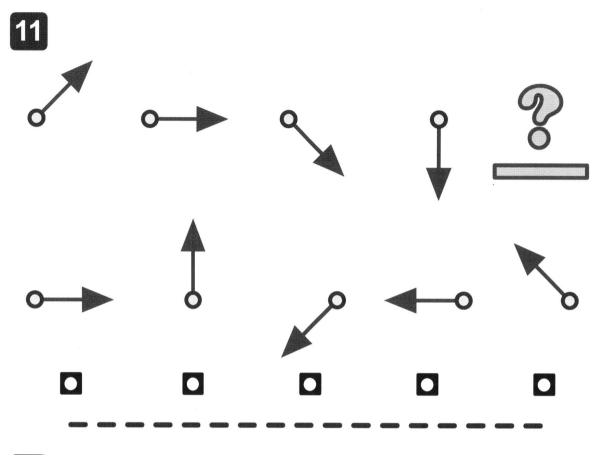

12

Dd Ee Ff Gg ?

Ff Ii Hh Jj Gg

Picture and Figure Series

13

14

15

 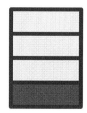 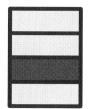 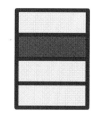

 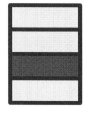 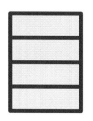 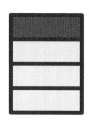 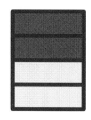

16

1   2

3   4   3   3

17

18

19

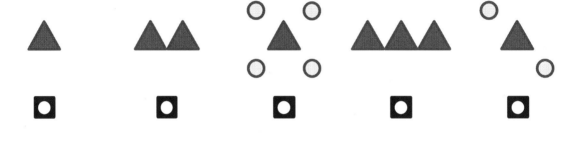

20

21

- - - - - - - - - - - - - - - - -

22

23

24

25

26

27

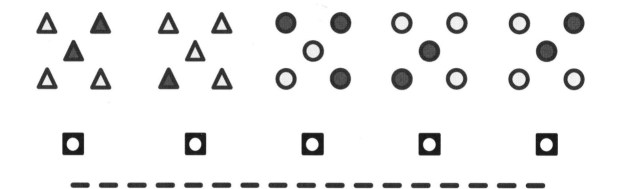

28

29

- - - - - - - - - - - - - - - - - -

30

31

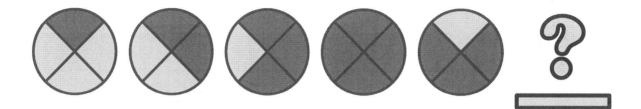

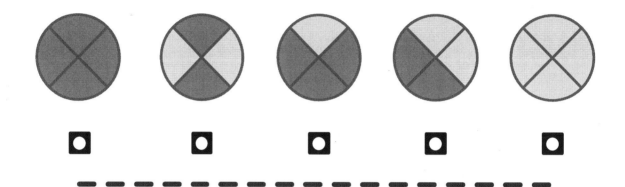

32

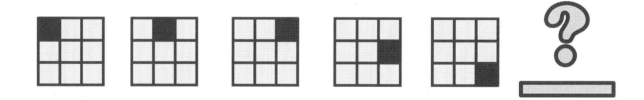

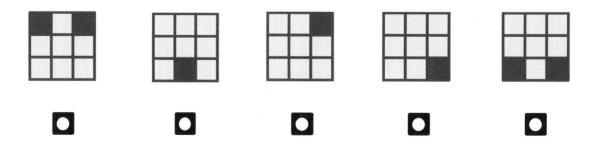

Picture and Figure Series

33

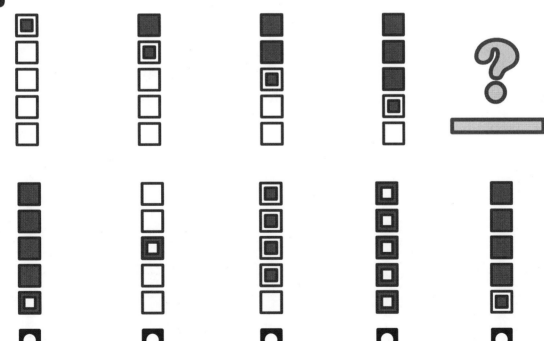

35

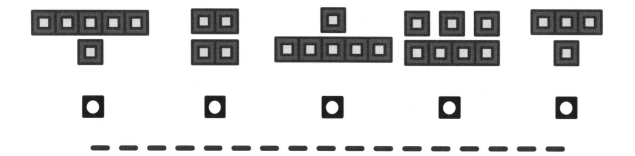

- -

36

Picture and Figure Series

37

38

39

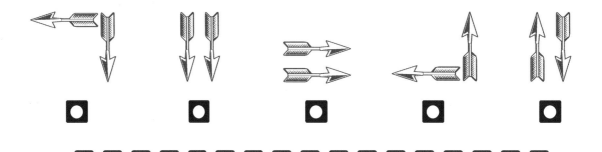

40

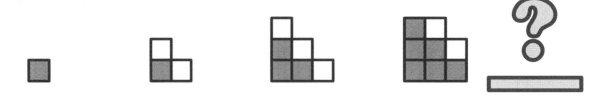

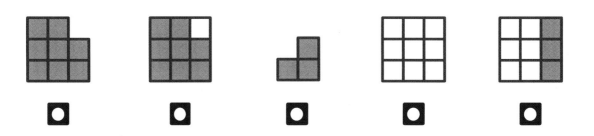

Picture and Figure Series Bright Kids NYC Inc ©

41

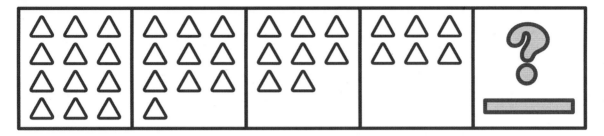

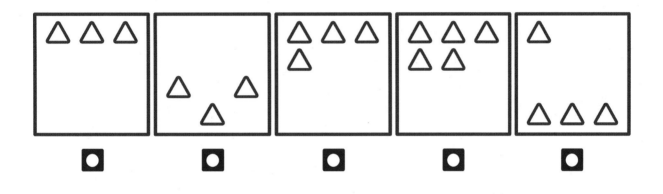

42

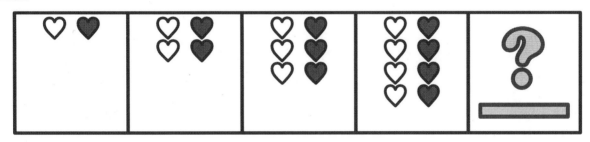

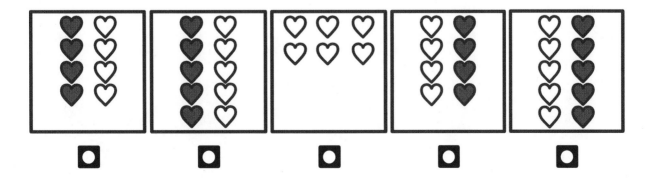

Picture and Figure Series

43

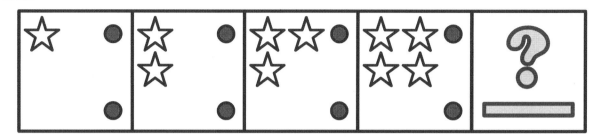

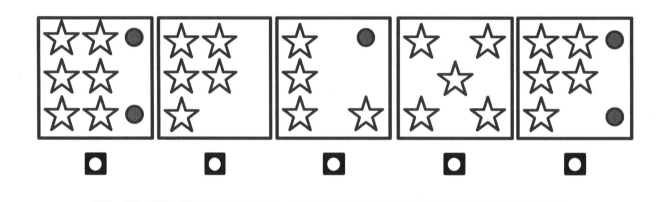

- -

44

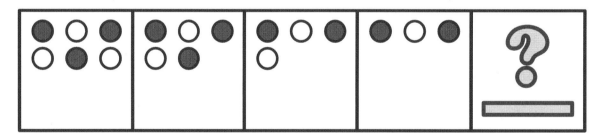

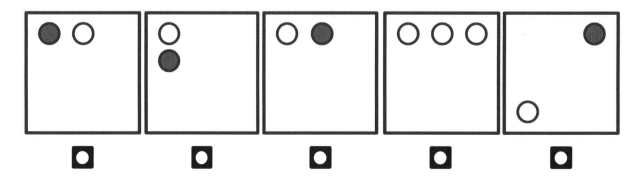

Picture and Figure Series

45

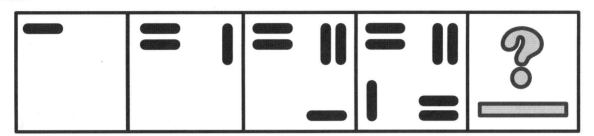

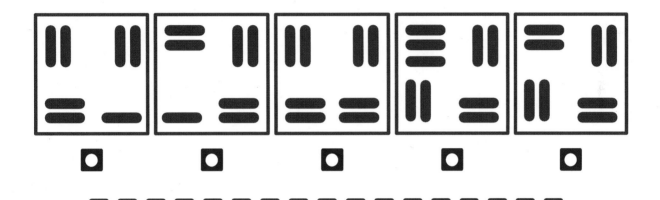

46

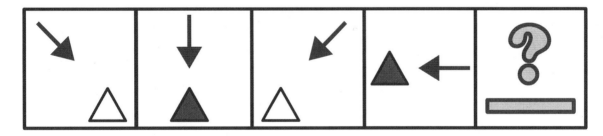

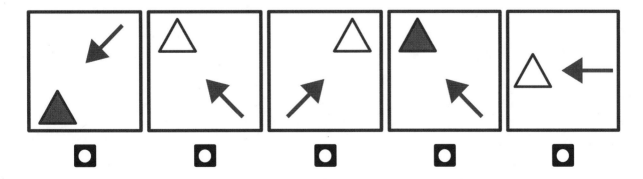

47

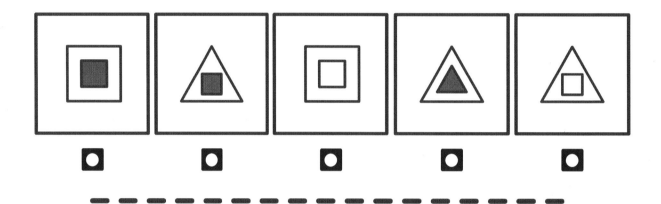

- - - - - - - - - - - - - - - - - - - -

48

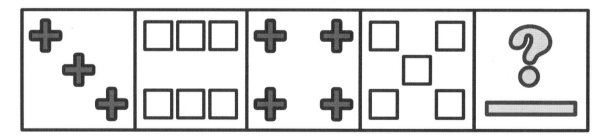

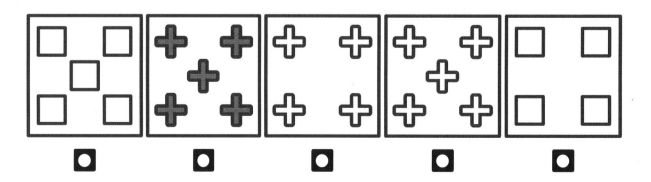

Picture and Figure Series Bright Kids NYC Inc ©

49

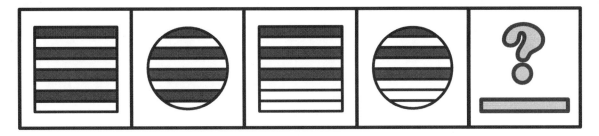

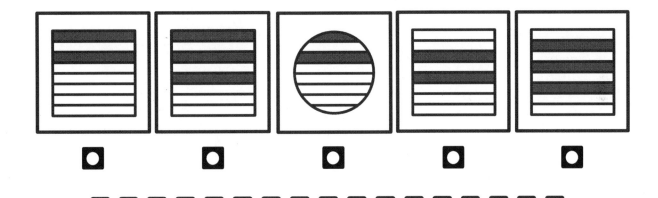

50

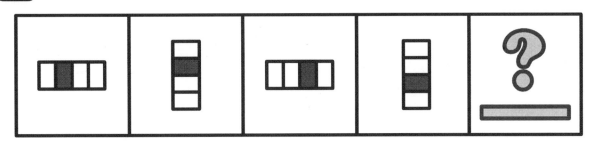

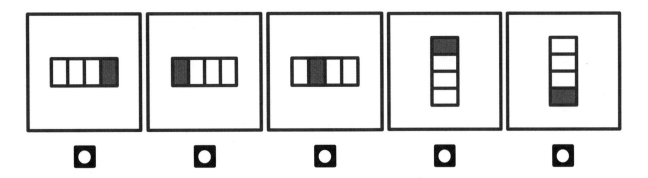

Picture and Figure Series

Section Three

Answer Keys

Picture and Figure Series

Picture Series Answer Key

NUMBER	CORRECT ANSWER	CHILD'S ANSWER
1.	5	
2.	2	
3.	1	
4.	2	
5.	5	
6.	2	
7.	2	
8.	2	
9.	1	
10.	1	
11.	5	
12.	2	
13.	5	
14.	3	
15.	3	
16.	3	
17.	3	
18.	4	
19.	1	
20.	2	
21.	2	
22.	1	
23.	2	
24.	5	
25.	4	
26.	5	
27.	1	
28.	3	
29.	4	
30.	1	

Figure Series Answer Key

NUMBER	CORRECT ANSWER	CHILD'S ANSWER
1.	5	
2.	3	
3.	5	
4.	3	
5.	2	
6.	4	
7.	4	
8.	2	
9.	1	
10.	2	
11.	3	
12.	3	
13.	5	
14.	4	
15.	4	
16.	1	
17.	4	
18.	2	
19.	4	
20.	1	
21.	5	
22.	1	
23.	2	
24.	2	
25.	1	
26.	4	
27.	1	
28.	2	
29.	5	
30.	5	
31.	4	
32.	2	
33.	1	
34.	5	

Figure Series Answer Key (Continued)

NUMBER	CORRECT ANSWER	CHILD'S ANSWER
35.	3	
36.	4	
37.	3	
38.	3	
39.	3	
40.	2	
41.	3	
42.	5	
43.	5	
44.	1	
45.	4	
46.	2	
47.	1	
48.	2	
49.	1	
50.	3	